THE MAGIC OF GREEN

The Color Books are dedicated to the Rainbow Child in all of you

Series concept by Ayman Sawaf
Copyright © 1995 by Enchanté Publishing
MRS. MURGATROYD Character copyright © 1993 by Enchanté
MRS. MURGATROYD™ is a trademark of Enchanté

Written by Neysa Griffith.
Character created by Steven Duarte.
Illustrated by Deborah Morse.
Edited by Gudrun Höy, Anne Sheldon and Linda Hull.
Book design by Romney Lange.

Enchanté Publishing
P.O. Box 620471
Woodside, CA 94062

Printed in Singapore

Library of Congress Cataloging-in-Publication Data
Griffith, Neysa
The magic of green / written by Neysa Griffith; character created by Steven Duarte; illustrated by Deborah Morse. - Ist ed.
    p.   cm.
Summary: Playful verses and illustrations invite children to enter the magical world of colors.
ISBN 1-56844-028-6 : $6.95
1. Green—Juvenile poetry. 2. Colors—Juvenile poetry.
3. Children's poetry. American [1. Green—Poetry. 2. American poetry.]
I. Neysa Griffith.   II. Morse, Deborah, ill.   III. Title.
PS3557.R4893M28   1995
811' .54—dc20   93-34811

First Edition
10 9 8 7 6 5 4 3 2 1

THE MAGIC OF
GREEN

Written by Neysa Griffith
Illustrated by Deborah Morse

enchanté Publishing

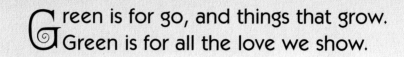

Green is for go, and things that grow.
Green is for all the love we show.

The power of green is the power to heal.
Green is for all the love we feel.

Apples, pears and sour limes,
green grapes grow on creeping vines.
Broccoli, peas and spinach, too.
All these greens are good for you.

A happy tune, a merry rhyme,
green is ever feeling fine.

Evergreen, giant pine,
mistletoe at Christmas time.

Forest green, the mighty oak,
protector of the woodland folk.

Little green elves and little green gnomes
live happily in their mushroom homes.

Laughing, leaping leprechauns
with deep green coats and stockings on.

Holding hands they laugh and sing,
dancing in the fairy ring.

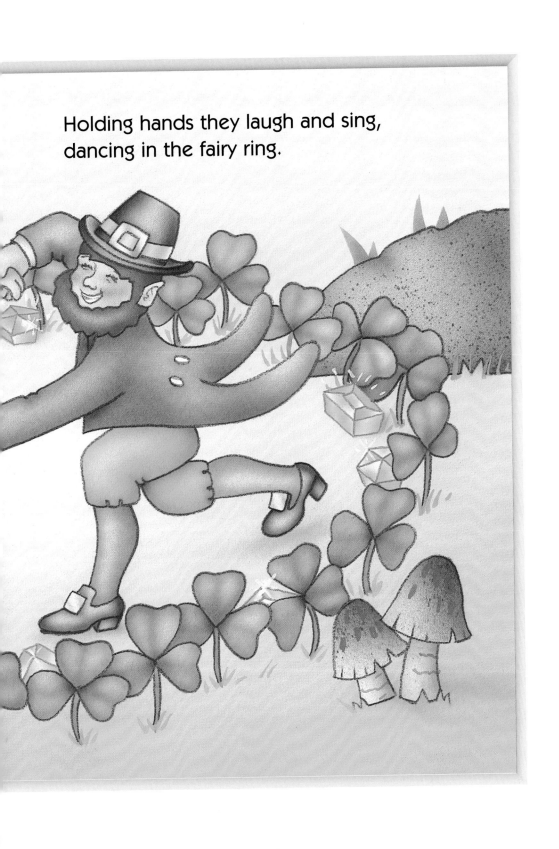

Barefoot in the park we walk.
Heart to heart we have a talk.
Green is the dream tomorrow brings;
the place where hope eternal springs.

Mermaids living in the sea
are just as real as you and me.

Pearly-finned with skin so fair,
sitting in a clam shell chair,
taking special time and care
to beachcomb out their waves of hair.

In the pond a big green frog
hops from lily pad to log.

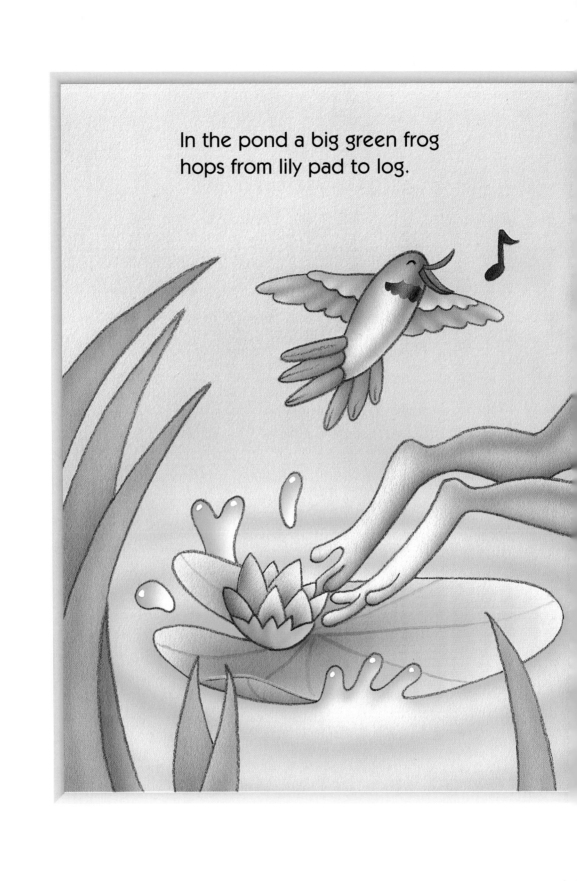

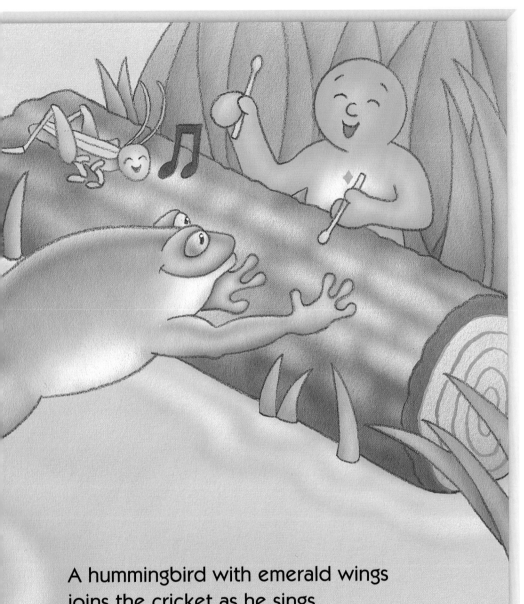

A hummingbird with emerald wings
joins the cricket as he sings
a sunny summer serenade,
echoing throughout the glade.

Giving the farmers a helping hand,
digging the dirt and tilling the land.

With seeds of every shape and size,
what they'll become, now that's the surprise.

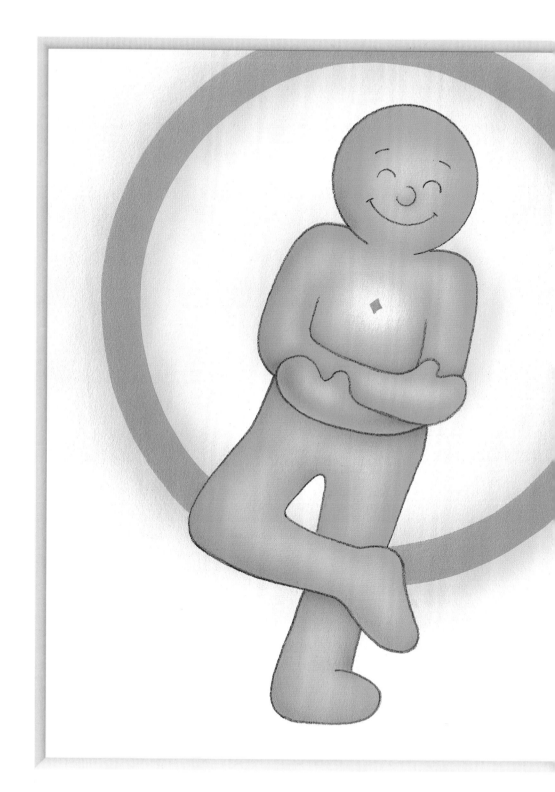

The magic of green lives inside of you.
It can happily help you in all that you do.
To make green your friend,
close your eyes and pretend...

You're sitting upon a leafy throne
in a tree house of your very own.
Below lies the garden of earthly delight,
a paradise of sound and sight.
Climb through the branches covered in fruits,
down to the moist, green, moss-covered roots.

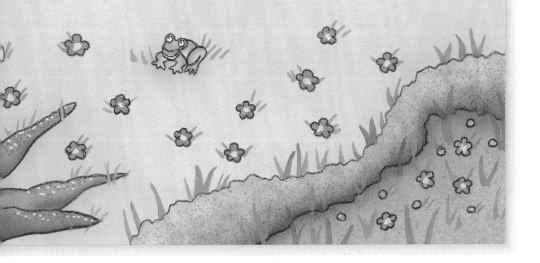

Plant your love and watch it grow.
See how far it lets you go.
Living with nature in harmony.
Tell the whole world, "I love to be me!"

Enchanté books are dedicated to enhancing the general
well-being of children by encouraging them to use their own
imagination and creativity to explore their thoughts and feelings.
Each story is a symbolic journey into the magical world of self,
where children discover the power they have within. Enchanté
offers high quality hardcover picture books with accompanying
activity books and parents' guides which include:

And Peter Said Goodbye
Exploring Grief
Exploring Grief With Your Child

Painting the Fire
Exploring Anger
Exploring Anger With Your Child

Red Poppies for a Little Bird
Exploring Guilt
Exploring Guilt With Your Child

The Rainbow Fields
Exploring Loneliness
Exploring Loneliness With Your Child

Nightmares in the Mist
Exploring Fear
Exploring Fear With Your Child

William's Gift
Exploring Hurt
Exploring Hurt With Your Child

Knight-time for Brigitte

For more information call:
1-800-473-2363

or (415) 529-2100
fax # (415) 851-2229